NATIONAL GEOGRAPHIC

Soil

George Wong

Contents

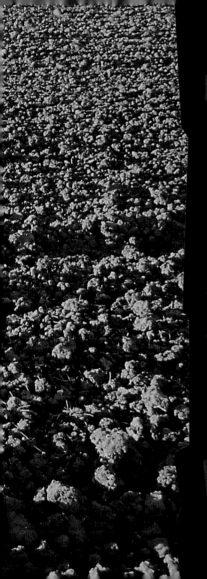

What is soil?

The land is covered with a layer of dirt.

This dirt is called soil.

Soil can be sandy.

Soil can be rocky.

Soil can be like clay.

Do you know how soil is made?

How is soil made?

It takes a very long time for soil to be made.

Soil is made from pieces of rock.

The pieces of rock are mixed with animals and plants that have died and rotted.

Some rocks lie on top of the ground.

Rain falls on them.

Snow and ice cover them.

The wind blows them.

After a long time, the water, the cold

and the wind help break the rocks into pieces.

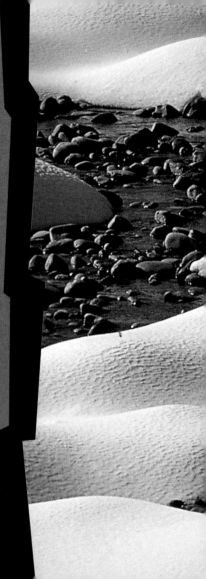

These pieces of rock then break
into smaller and smaller pieces.
After thousands of years, the tiny pieces
of rock become soil.

Rocks get smaller and smaller over time.

Plants and animals also help make soil.

Fallen leaves and dead plants
lie on the ground.

When animals die, their bodies
also lie on the ground.

Hot sun shines on them.

Cold rain falls on them.

Snow and ice cover them.

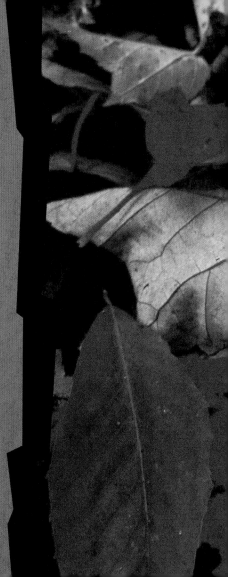

After a long time, the heat, the water
and the cold help make the leaves
and bodies rot into the ground.
The rotting leaves and bodies
help make the soil rich with nutrients.
When the soil is rich with nutrients,
plants can grow there.

Leaves and bodies rot into the ground.

Who needs soil?

Most plants need soil to live.

Plants have roots that reach down into the soil.

The roots spread out.

The soil helps plants stand up.

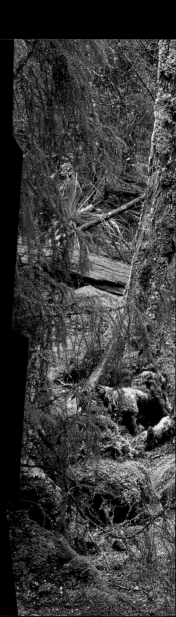

The roots reach down into the soil.

Plants get some of their food and water from the soil.

Their roots collect the food and water that help the plants grow.

Without soil, most plants could not grow.

Plants need soil.

Animals need soil to live, too.

Some animals eat plants.

Other animals eat the animals

that eat plants.

Without soil, most plants could not grow.

Without plants, animals would have

nothing to eat.

Animals need soil.

People need soil to live, too.
We use the soil to grow plants
that we can eat.
We feed plants to animals
that we can eat.

Without soil, most plants could not grow.

Without plants, animals would have

nothing to eat.

Without plants and animals,

people would have nothing to eat.

People need soil.

Glossary

clay   stiff, sticky dirt

nutrients   food necessary for things to grow

rich   full of good things

roots   part of a plant that grows under the ground

rot   break down into smaller pieces